CW00405048

by Iain Gray

Lang**Syne**
PUBLISHING
WRITING *to* REMEMBER

LangSyne

PUBLISHING

WRITING *to* REMEMBER

79 Main Street, Newtongrange,
Midlothian EH22 4NA
Tel: 0131 344 0414   Fax: 0845 075 6085
E-mail: info@lang-syne.co.uk
www.langsyneshop.co.uk

Design by Dorothy Meikle
Printed by Printwell Ltd
© Lang Syne Publishers Ltd 2018

ISBN 978-1-85217-421-7

Hill

MOTTO:
Advance.

CREST:
A castellated tower.

NAME variations include:
Hille
Hills
Hyll

*Echoes of a far distant past
can still be found in most names*

Chapter one:

Origins of Scottish surnames

by George Forbes

It all began with the Normans.

For it was they who introduced surnames into common usage more than a thousand years ago, initially based on the title of their estates, local villages and chateaux in France to distinguish and identify these landholdings, usually acquired at the point of a bloodstained sword.

Such grand descriptions also helped enhance the prestige of these arrogant warlords and generally glorify their lofty positions high above the humble serfs slaving away below in the pecking order who only had single names, often with Biblical connotations as in Pierre and Jacques.

The only descriptive distinctions among this peasantry concerned their occupations, like Pierre the swineherd or Jacques the ferryman.

The Normans themselves were originally Vikings (or Northmen) who raided, colonised and eventually settled down around the French coastline.

They had sailed up the Seine in their longboats in 900 AD under their ferocious leader Rollo and ruled the roost in north east France before sailing over to conquer England, bringing their relatively new tradition of having surnames with them.

It took another hundred years for the Normans to percolate northwards and surnames did not begin to appear in Scotland until the thirteenth century.

These adventurous knights brought an aura of chivalry with them and it was said no damsel of any distinction would marry a man unless he had at least two names.

The family names included that of Scotland's great hero Robert De Brus and his compatriots were warriors from families like the De Morevils, De Umphravils, De Berkelais, De Quincis, De Viponts and De Vaux.

As the knights settled the boundaries of their vast estates, they took territorial names, as in Hamilton, Moray, Crawford, Cunningham, Dunbar, Ross, Wemyss, Dundas, Galloway, Renfrew, Greenhill, Hazelwood, Sandylands and Church-hill.

Other names, though not with any obvious geographical or topographical features, nevertheless derived from ancient parishes like Douglas, Forbes, Dalyell and Guthrie.

Other surnames were coined in connection with occupations, castles or legendary deeds. Stuart originated in the word steward, a prestigious post which was an integral part of any large medieval household. The same applied to Cooks, Chamberlains, Constables and Porters.

Borders towns and forts – needed in areas like the Debateable Lands which were constantly fought over by feuding local families – had their own distinctive names; and it was often from them that the resident groups took their communal titles, as in the Grahams of Annandale, the Elliots and Armstrongs of the East Marches, the Scotts and Kerrs of Teviotdale and Eskdale.

Even physical attributes crept into surnames, as in Small, Little and More (the latter being 'beg' in Gaelic), Long or Lang, Stark, Stout, Strong or Strang and even Jolly.

Mieklejohns would have had the strength of several men, while Littlejohn was named after the legendary sidekick of Robin Hood.

Colours got into the act with Black, White, Grey, Brown and Green (Red developed into Reid,

Ruddy or Ruddiman). Blue was rare and nobody ever wanted to be associated with yellow.

Pompous worthies took the name Wiseman, Goodman and Goodall.

Words intimating the sons of leading figures were soon affiliated into the language as in Johnson, Adamson, Richardson and Thomson, while the Norman equivalent of Fitz (from the French-Latin 'filius' meaning 'son') cropped up in Fitzmaurice and Fitzgerald.

The prefix 'Mac' was 'son of' in Gaelic and clans often originated with occupations – as in MacNab being sons of the Abbot, MacPherson and MacVicar being sons of the minister and MacIntosh being sons of the chief.

The church's influence could be found in the names Kirk, Clerk, Clarke, Bishop, Friar and Monk. Proctor came from a church official, Singer and Sangster from choristers, Gilchrist and Gillies from Christ's servant, Mitchell, Gilmory and Gilmour from servants of St Michael and Mary, Malcolm from a servant of Columba and Gillespie from a bishop's servant.

The rudimentary medical profession was represented by Barber (a trade which also once included dentistry and surgery) as well as Leech or Leitch.

Businessmen produced Merchants, Mercers, Monypennies, Chapmans, Sellers and Scales, while down at the old village watermill the names that cropped up included Miller, Walker and Fuller.

Other self explanatory trades included Coopers, Brands, Barkers, Tanners, Skinners, Brewsters and Brewers, Tailors, Saddlers, Wrights, Cartwrights, Smiths, Harpers, Joiners, Sawyers, Masons and Plumbers.

Even the scenery was utilised as in Craig, Moor, Hill, Glen, Wood and Forrest.

Rank, whether high or low, took its place with Laird, Barron, Knight, Tennant, Farmer, Husband, Granger, Grieve, Shepherd, Shearer and Fletcher.

The hunt and the chase supplied Hunter, Falconer, Fowler, Fox, Forrester, Archer and Spearman.

The renowned medieval historian Froissart, who eulogised about the romantic deeds of chivalry (and who condemned Scotland as being a poverty stricken wasteland), once sniffily dismissed the peasantry of his native France as the jacquerie (or the jacques-without-names) but it was these same humble folk who ended up overthrowing the arrogant aristocracy.

In the olden days, only the blueblooded knights of antiquity were entitled to full, proper names, both Christian and surnames, but with the passing of time and a more egalitarian, less feudal atmosphere, more respectful and worthy titles spread throughout the populace as a whole.

Echoes of a far distant past can still be found in most names and they can be borne with pride in commemoration of past generations who fought and toiled in some capacity or other to make our nation what it now is, for good or ill.

Chapter two:

Honour bound

A 'location surname' in that it originates with reference to someone who lived on a hill or where a hill was a dominant feature of the local landscape, 'Hill' is ranked at 30 in the list of the 100 most common surnames in the United Kingdom.

Not specific to any particular region of Scotland, where it is ranked at number 93, it nevertheless appears to have been commonly found in the Lowlands, with bearers of the name not recognised as a sept, or sub-branch, of any particular Scottish clan.

There are, however, a number of Hill family Coats of Arms, with the most common motto recognised as "Advance" and crest of a castellated tower.

In common with several other common surnames found in Scotland, lack of a definite clan connection does not preclude them from having made a significant contribution to the vibrant drama that is the nation's history.

Scottish bearers of the Hill name were also largely responsible for introducing the name to

Ireland, although it is also sometimes found on the island as a variant of the native Irish names Glanney and Glenny.

The introduction of the name to the Emerald Isle from Scotland, mainly to the northern province of Ulster, came about through 'plantation'.

This was a policy that involved the settlement of loyal Protestants throughout the reigns of England's Elizabeth I, James I (James VI of Scotland) and Charles I.

One bearer of the Hill name figures in the grim accounts of one of the most notorious incidents in Scotland's frequently bloody history.

This was the infamous Massacre of Glencoe.

Although a Jacobite rebellion had been quashed in 1689, one year after James II (James VII of Scotland) had fled to exile in France and William of Orange had been invited to take the united thrones of England and Scotland, the Highlands were still in a ferment of unrest.

The problem faced by the authorities was how to quell this unrest and pacify the clans that still adhered to the forlorn Jacobite cause.

A meeting of clan chiefs was convened near Bridge of Orchy, in Perthshire, in June of 1691, and all clans that had fought against the government were granted an amnesty on condition that their chiefs signed a personal oath of allegiance to William, before a magistrate, no later than January 1, 1692.

The Secretary of State for Scotland, Sir John Dalrymple, the Master of Stair, was convinced that not all of the clan chiefs would sign the required oath, and accordingly laid plans to punish those who refused.

As a result of circumstances that were beyond his control, not the least heavy snowfalls that slowed his progress, Alasdair MacIain, the 12th Clan Chief of the Glencoe MacDonalds, was late in meeting the required deadline.

This ominously resulted in his name not being entered on the all-important list of those who had signed.

The Master of Stair saw his opportunity and resolved to make a harsh example of the MacDonalds of Glencoe.

A secret commission to carry this out was given to Captain Robert Campbell of Glenlyon, who took a force of about 140 men to Glencoe, armed with a warrant to quarter them in the homes of the MacDonalds who lived at the bottom of the glen.

Glenlyon and his soldiers spent nearly two weeks enjoying the hospitality of the 500 or so MacDonalds among whom they had been quartered.

Orders finally arrived for Glenlyon to fall upon the unsuspecting MacDonalds and massacre them – sparing no one under the age of 70, women and children not excepted.

The exact figure is not known, but in the early hours of February 13, 1692, at least 38 men, women, and children were slaughtered while countless others died in the severe snowstorm into which they had fled.

MacIain of Glencoe was cold-bloodedly shot as he attempted to rise from his bed.

One of the very few to have played an honourable role in this otherwise sordid affair and to have emerged with his character unblemished, was Colonel John Hill, who served as Governor of Fort William from 1690 to 1698.

Despite the role he played, surprisingly very little biographical detail is available, but what is known is that he was of a family of Hill who owned an estate at Waughton, near East Fortune, and that at the time of the massacre the Scot was also a Lieutenant Colonel in the Earl of Argyle's Regiment of Foot.

Described by one source as "an honest old

soldier", it was before him that the ill-fated MacDonald appeared at Fort William to take the oath.

But Colonel Hill had to explain to the exhausted Clan Chief that only the sheriff at Inveraray could take it and, sympathising with his plight, provided him with a letter to the sheriff urgently appealing that he be granted some leniency over his late arrival.

Unfortunately this had no effect, and matters proceeded on their grim course.

After the massacre, it was thanks only to Hill that the survivors were pardoned and allowed to return to what remained of their dwellings.

This was because of a personal appeal he made on their behalf to the King.

As the records note: " … on the solicitation of Colonel Hill, His Majesty granted pardon and remission to the people of Glencoe, allowing them liberty to return and dwell in their old habitations, upon the condition that, for the future, they shall carry themselves peaceably, honestly and abiding by the laws …"

On a much different field of conflict, bearers of the Hill name gained honours and distinction during the American Civil War of 1861 to 1865.

Born in 1825 in Culpeper, Virginia, Ambrose Powell Hill, better known as A.P. Hill, was the Confederate general famed for his command of Hill's Light Division of the Army of North Virginia.

Distinguishing himself in battles that included Second Bull Run, Antietam and Fredericksburg, he was killed in April 1865 during the siege of Petersburg.

The sword he was wielding when he fell is now on display at the Chesterfield County Museum, Virginia, while Fort A.P. Hill, in Virginia's Caroline County, is named in his honour.

One of his contemporaries in the Army of North Virginia was the Confederate general Daniel Harvey Hill, better known as D. H. Hill.

Born in 1821 of Scots-Irish stock in York District, South Carolina, he was also a noted scholar.

Surviving the Civil War, he later edited the North Carolina magazine *The Land We Love*, dealing with historical and social subjects, while he served from 1877 until five years before his death in 1889 as the first president of the University of Arkansas.

Chapter three:

Teachers and tycoons

Back in one of the Hill homelands of Scotland, and away from the battlefield, George Hill was the outspoken Church of Scotland minister who held a number of distinguished positions in the religious life of the nation.

Born the son of a minister in St Andrews in 1750 and following in his father's footsteps by being ordained a minister himself in 1778, he served as Moderator of the General Assembly of the Church of Scotland in 1789 and held a number of other positions that included principal of Mary's College, St Andrews, and Dean of the Chapel Royal, Edinburgh.

Despite his reputation as an ardent British patriot, he was vociferously opposed during the French Revolutionary Wars to a proposal that ministers should preach in support of a financial levy from parishioners in aid of the war effort.

This, he said, would compromise the independence of the Church, and famously declared that, while he would willingly contribute himself, he would "strip the gown from my back rather than obey an order to promote it from the pulpit." Also a noted teacher and a founding member of the Royal Society of Edinburgh, he died in 1810.

Not only a noted artist but also a pioneer of early photographic techniques, David Octavius Hill was born in 1802 in Perth, the son of a publisher and bookseller.

Educated at Perth Academy and later studying at the School of Design, Edinburgh, where he learned the art of lithography, he first came to attention through his *Sketches of Scenery in Perthshire*, while The Institution for the Promotion of Fine Arts in Scotland exhibited many of his landscape paintings.

Among a number of Scottish artists who became dissatisfied with the work of the institution, he helped to found an alternative, the Scottish Academy, later the Royal Scottish Academy, in 1829.

In addition to providing illustrations for the works of Robert Burns and Sir Walter Scott, he also collaborated from 1839 with the pioneering photographer Robert Adamson in producing a stunning series of prints that utilised the latter's skill in photography and Hill's adeptness in composition.

One of the most famous examples of their collaboration is *The Disruption*, based on the

Disruption Assembly in Edinburgh in 1843 when a number of Church of Scotland ministers walked out of the assembly hall in protest and founded the Free Church of Scotland.

Hill and Adamson are also famed for a number of portraits of famous Edinburgh citizens and other Scots luminaries that had the tombs of Greyfriars Kirkyard as a backdrop.

It was in this kirkyard that a National Covenant, pledging defence of the Presbyterian religion, was signed in February of 1638.

Also a secretary to the Royal Scottish Academy (RSA), Hill died in 1870 and is buried in Edinburgh's Dean Cemetery.

Scottish bearers of the Hill name have also thrived far from their native land as entrepreneurs, making a significant contribution to the nations in which they settled.

Not the least of these was John Hill, born in 1824 in Old Monklands, now part of Coatbridge, Lanarkshire.

Immigrating to the United States at the age of 20, he later settled in Baton Rouge, Louisiana, where his Scots-born uncle, Alexander Christie, owned a coalmine.

But, rather than entering his uncle's business, he started an iron foundry in Baton Rouge and also operated a sawmill on the banks of the Mississippi and a ferry.

Marrying Catherine McPhail, originally from Glasgow, in 1851, the couple settled in a magnificent mansion in Baton Rouge's Lafayette Street, while Hill also expanded his business interests by buying a sugar plantation.

It was the John Hill Foundry that built the imposing 1575ft. long cast-iron fence for the State of Louisiana's state capitol building in Baton Rouge – a fence that was carefully repaired in 2009 in view of its historic importance.

His legacy also survives in the form of the Hill Memorial Library at Louisiana State University, founded by Hill, who died in 1910, in memory of his son, John Hill Jr.

Known as "The Empire Builder", James Jerome Hill was the Canadian-American railroad tycoon who was born in 1838 in Eramosa Township, Ontario. Despite having had only nine years of formal education, he became chief executive of a number of railroad lines that came under the 'umbrella' of the Great Northern Railway.

This railroad empire, also known as the Hill Lines, covered a vast area that took in much of North America's Upper Midwest, the Pacific Northwest and the northern Great Plains.

He died in 1916, and his heirs later established the James J. Hill Reference Library in St Paul, Minnesota.

Considered a premier source for publicly accessible business information in the United States, it now also boasts a number of online programmes that can be accessed by small business owners worldwide.

A great patron of the arts, one of Hill's other legacies is his art collection now housed in the Minneapolis Institute of Arts.

On British shores, the mathematician Thomas Hill was part of a family dynasty of bearers of the name. Born in 1763 in Kidderminster, Worcestershire, he is credited with having invented the Single Transferable Vote (STV) system of proportional representation – first used in 1840 for election to Australia's Adelaide City Council.

He died in 1851, and one of his sons was the British postal service reformer Sir Rowland Hill.

Born in 1795 in Kidderminster, it was through his appointment to reorganise the Post Office that he revolutionised the system by introducing the Uniform Penny Post and, in 1840, the adhesive postage stamp, which had been invented earlier.

Also a noted social reformer, he died in 1879 and is interred in Westminster Abbey.

There is a statue of him in London's King Edward Street, while the Rowland Hill Awards, started in 1997 by the Royal Mail and the British Philatelic Trust, are awarded annually for philatelic innovation, initiative and enterprise.

His older brother, Edwin Hill, was also a postal reformer.

Born in 1793, he served, from 1840 to 1872, as the first British Controller of Stamps and was responsible in 1851 for the invention of the first mechanical system to make envelopes – the patent for which was later bought by Walter de la Rue.

Also a campaigner for Parliamentary reform, he died in 1876.

Renowned as Victorian-era social reformers, Miranda Hill and her sister Octavia were born in Wisbech, Cambridgeshire in, respectively, 1836 and 1838.

Octavia, concerned with the housing conditions of the urban poor, became a leading campaigner for the development of 'social housing' in suburban areas, while along with Miranda was instrumental in the foundation in 1876 of the Kyrle Society.

With the aim of "bringing art, books, music and open spaces into the lives of the urban poor", the society is recognised as having provided the blueprint in 1896 for the foundation of the National Trust.

Miranda Hill died in 1910, while Octavia, who was also a member of the Royal Commission on Poor Laws, died two years later.

Chapter four:

On the world stage

Bearers of the Hill name have excelled, and continue to excel, through a colourful range of pursuits.

Best known internationally for his role as King Theoden in the 2002 *The Lord of the Rings: The Two Towers* and in the 2003 *The Lord of the Rings: The Return of the King*, **Bernard Hill** is the British actor of stage, television and film who was born in 1944 in Blackley, Manchester.

First coming to prominence through his role as Yosser Hughes in the 1979 Alan Bleasdale television Play for Today, *The Black Stuff*, and its sequel, *Boys from the Blackstuff*, he has also appeared in films that include the 1982 *Ghandi* and the 2008 *Valkyrie*.

Born in 1964 in Encino, Los Angeles, Dana Lynne Goetz was the American actress better known as **Dana Hill** – with Hill being her mother's maiden name.

Her distinctive raspy voice and childlike appearance allowed her to play adolescent roles right up until her death in 1996, at the age of 32.

Best known for her role as Audrey Griswold in the 1983 *National Lampoon's European Vacation*, from 1987 she provided the voice for Scrappy, the orphaned mouse, in episodes of *Mighty Mouse: The New Adventures*.

Married to British actor Sean Bean from 1990 to 1997, **Melanie Hill** is the actress who was born in 1962 in Sunderland.

Films in which she has appeared include the 2007 *Stardust* and, from 2009, *White Girl*, while she also for a time played the role of Aveline in the popular British sitcom *Bread*.

Also on the British television screen, **Harry Hill**, born Matthew Keith Hill in 1964 in Woking, Surrey is the award-winning comedian, television presenter and author who is also a qualified medical doctor.

First coming to attention with his radio show *Harry Hill's Fruit Corner*, his many awards include BAFTAs in both 2008 and 2009 for his *Harry Hill's TV Burp* for, respectively, Best Entertainment Performance and Best Entertainment Programme.

Also in the field of comedy, **Benny Hill**, born Alfred Hawthorne Hill in Southampton in 1924, was the popular comedian and actor best known for his iconic *Benny Hill Show*, which ran on and off on British television from 1957 until as late as 1989.

One of his many fans was Charlie Chaplin,

and in 1991, fourteen years after Chaplin's death, he won the coveted Charlie Chaplin International Award for Comedy – a year before his own death.

His comedy single *Ernie (The Fastest Milkman in the West)* was a No. 1 hit in Britain in 1971, while films in which he appeared include the 1965 *Those Magnificent Men in Their Flying Machines* and the 1969 *The Italian Job*.

Bearers of the Hill name have also excelled in the highly competitive world of sport, and no less so than on the motor racing circuit.

Born in 1929 in Hampstead, London, **Graham Hill** was the British racing driver who twice won the Formula One World Championship. His early interest was motorcycle racing, and it was not until he was aged 24 that he passed his driving test.

He won his first Formula One World Championship only seven years later, followed by another win in 1968.

Also the winner in 1966 of the Indianapolis 500 and, with Henri Pescarolo, the 1972 Le Mans 24 Hours, and the 1969 Monaco Grand Prix and other races, he was among six people killed when their light aircraft crashed while attempting to land in thick fog near a golf course in north London, in November of 1975.

Inducted into the International Motorsports Hall of Fame in 1990, he was the father of **Damon Hill**, born in 1960, and who, following in father's tyre tracks, was the winner of the 1996 Australian Grand Prix.

Yet another father and son motor racing pair, **Phil Hill**, born in 1927 in Miami and who died in 2008, is the only American driver to date to have won, in 1961, the Formula One World Championship, while his son, **Derek Hill**, born in 1975, was the winner of the 1995 Ferrari Challenge International.

In the Canadian national sport of ice hockey, **Brian Hill**, born in 1957 in Saskatchewan, is the former right-winger who, during a playing career that lasted from 1977 to 1988, played for teams that include the Hartford Whalers, Atlanta Flames and New England Whalers.

Later obtaining Austrian citizenship, he played for Austria in the 1986 and 1987 World Championships.

On the fields of European football, **Jimmy Hill** was the English football personality born in 1928 in Balham, London, and who died in 2015.

Not only a football commentator, in his time he was also a player, coach, manager and chairman of the Professional Footballers' Association.

Teams he played for include Brentford and, from 1952 to 1961, Fulham, while he was manager of Coventry City from 1961 to 1967.

In his role as football commentator, he was the figure who Scotland fans, known as the Tartan Army, loved to hate.

This followed his dismissive description of a Scottish player's goal against Brazil during the 1982 World Cup as a 'toe-poke', a remark for which he later apologised.

He was also renowned for match comments that include: "If England are going to win this match, they're going to have to score a goal", and "That's a wise substitution…three fresh men, three fresh legs."

In baseball, **Aaron Hill**, born in 1982 in Visalia, California, is the All-Star Major League player whose many awards and honours include two Fielding Bible Awards for fielding excellence.

On the athletics track, **Albert Hill**, born in 1899 in Tooting, London, and who later immigrated to Canada, won a gold medal for the 800-metres and gold for the 1500-metres at the 1920 Olympics in Antwerp; he died in 1969.

From sport to the creative world of music, **Alfred Hill**, born in 1869 in Melbourne, Australia, and who also spent part of his career in New Zealand, was the composer, conductor and teacher who, in 1913, was a co-founder of the Australian Opera League, and, later, the Sydney Repertory Theatre Society.

Also a co-founder of the New South Wales State Conservatorium of Music and responsible for more than 500 compositions, he died in 1960, the same year in which he was made a Companion of the Order of St Michael and St George.

In a different musical genre, **Andrew Hill**, born in Chicago in 1931, was the American jazz pianist and composer whose albums include the 1968 *Grass Roots*, the 1990 *But Not Farewell* and, released a year before his death in 2006, *Time Lines*.

Born in 1889 in Boston, **Billy Hill** was the prolific American writer of cowboy songs and other genres that include *They Cut Down the Old Pine Tree*, *The Last Roundup*, *Wagon Wheels* and *Empty Saddles*.

One of his biggest hits was *The Glory of Love*, later covered by singers who include Peggy Lee, Dean Martin, Otis Redding and Bette Midler, while he also co-wrote what became the Elvis Presley hit, *That's When Your Heartaches Begin*. An inductee of the Songwriters Hall of Fame and the Nashville Songwriters Hall of Fame, he died in 1940.

In country music, Audrey Faith Perry is the top-selling American country singer better known as **Faith Hill**. Born in 1967 in Ridgeland, Mississippi, and married to fellow country singer Tim McGraw, her album *Breathe* won a 2001 Grammy Award for Best Country Music Album, while she also won the 2006 American Music Award for Favorite Country Female Artist.

Born in 1949 in Dallas, Texas, Joseph Michael Hill is the American bass guitarist and vocalist better known as **Dusty Hill** and who, along with Frank Beard and Billy Gibbon, is a member of the American rock band ZZ Top. Founded in 1969, their albums include the 1972 *Rio Grande Mud*, the 1981 *El Loco* and the 1985 *Afterburner*.

Best known for writing the book for the Broadway musical *The Story of My Life*, along with the composer Neil Bartram, **Brian Hill** is the Canadian actor, director and writer born in 1962 in Kitchener, Ontario.

Also in the world of the written word, **Reginald Hill**, born in 1936 in West Hartlepool, Co. Durham, is the English crime writer best known for his *Dalziel and Pascoe* series of novels, many of which have been adapted for television.

Also known for his *Joe Sixsmith* series of novels, he was the recipient in 1995 of the Crime Writers' Association Cartier Diamond Dagger for Lifetime Achievement.

Born in 1972 in Hermon, Maine, Joseph Hillstrom King is the American author and comic book writer better known as **Joe Hill**.

Author of novels that include the 2010 *Horns* and the recipient of a British Fantasy Award and a Bram Stoker Award for Best Fiction Collection, his parents are the horror writer Stephen King and fellow writer Tabitha King.

Born in Melbourne in 1942, **Anthony Hill** is the Australian author whose books include the 1998 *Birdsong* and the 2002 *Young Digger*.

Born in 1899 in Rockhampton, Queensland, **Ernestine Hill** was the Australian journalist and novelist whose books include her 1937 *The Great Loneliness* and her 1943 *My Love Must Wait*; she died in 1972.

From the written word to the sciences, **Archibald Hill**, born in 1886 in Bristol, was the English physiologist regarded as one of the founders of biophysics. Along with the German Otto Fritz Meyerhof, he shared a Nobel Prize in Physiology or

Medicine for his research on the production of mechanical work and heat in muscles.

Married to Margaret Keynes, a daughter of the eminent British economist John Maynard Keynes, he died in 1977, while their children include the leading economist Polly Hill, the physiologist David Keynes Hill and the child psychiatrist Janet Hill.

Digging up the past, Asa Thomas Hill, better known as **A.T. Hill**, born in 1871 in Cisne, Illinois, and who died in 1953, was the American businessman and self-taught archaeologist who, because of excavations he carried out in the 1930s and 1940s on Native American sites, is recognised as the father of systematic archaeology in Nebraska.

Two bearers of the Hill name with a rather unusual, and musical, claim to fame are the sisters **Patty** and **Mildred Hill**. Patty, born in 1868 near Louisville, Kentucky, and who died in 1946, had been a nursery school teacher when she collaborated with her sister in writing a song for her young pupils called *Good Morning to All*. Later adapted, it became the well-known *Happy Birthday to You*.

In was in recognition of the international popularity of the ditty that in 1996 the sisters were inducted into the Songwriters Hall of Fame.